FAITH
FOR A
SECULAR WORLD

FAITH
FOR A
SECULAR WORLD

by
MYRON S. AUGSBURGER

WORD BOOKS,
Publishers

Waco, Texas   —   London, England

FAITH FOR A SECULAR WORLD

LIBRARY OF CONGRESS CATALOG CARD NUMBER: 68-31104

Printed in the United States of America

To my wife's parents, Lloy and Elizabeth Kniss, whose commitment in faith and whose missionary spirit has enriched the lives
of many whom they served.

Contents

Preface 9

1. Faith Is Inescapable 13

2. True Religion Is Not A Crutch 17

3. Whole Persons 21

4. Understanding One's Self 27

5. Christ, the Center of Life 31

6. Freedom and Obedience 37

7. Educating the Conscience 41

8. Accepting God's Will 45

9. Prayer that Counts 49

10. Relating to Others Through Christ 53

11. My Brother's Keeper? 57

12. Forgiveness, Not Tolerance 61

13. Yes—As Big As Life 65

14. Joy in the Spirit 69

15. The Difficulties of Love 73

16. Justice, the Virtue of Wrath 77

17. Influence for Good 81

18. The Impact of Sanctity 85

19. Members of His Kingdom 89

20. Decision 93

Preface

Some years ago I read Dr. Glover's statement, "The early Church grew because it outlived, out-thought, and outdied everybody around." This is a challenge the twentieth century church must seek to measure up to. Living as a committed Christian in a modern world does not mean that one can escape facing the questions and the issues of our times. Relevance is not in changing the message of faith, but is relating faith to actual and current issues. As a committed Christian, I with you, am a modern. I am involved in a world that is undergoing the processes of secularization and change, not as a spectator but as a participant. With you I want to read clearly both God's world and God's Word. My thought has been enriched by evangelistic preaching missions in major cities, by numerous seminars with pastors from many denominations, and for the last five years by the dialogue and interchange with college students and faculty at Eastern Mennonite College and Seminary. It is my desire to make Christianity intelligible, desirable and visible.

The chapters of this book are presented as meditations on meaningful faith for a secular world. Much of what is presented is not new, although it may be arranged and expressed in a different form. I am grateful for the many lives that have enriched mine by Inter-Church work and relationships and have drawn from those experiences as well as from rather broad reading habits. Where I have quoted ideas by memory and have not been able to give credit for them, I here acknowledge my indebtedness to others and write in the spirit of sharing truths that have changed my life and have become a part of my understanding of the Gospel.

In the quest to understand faith, to have an intelligent basis for one's religious life, faith is presented in this treatise by putting the volitional first rather than the intellectual. This is simply the admission that what keeps men from believing in God is most often man's pride and his lack of a desire to know God rather than intellectual problems that are insurmountable. But it is my sincere hope that in some way I have coupled these two together so that faith can be seen as intelligent and reasonable. It is my prayer that the Spirit of God may guide the reader through these meditations as a sincere quest for wholeness of life. The value of the book is not in its style but in its spirit, and I present it to help others enjoy as I do the exhilaration of life in Christ.

—Myron S. Augsburger
Eastern Mennonite College
Harrisonburg, Virginia
September, 1968

Introduction

In today's society we face a crisis of values. The challenges before us question our shallow materialism, our assumed righteousness, and our future destiny. Confronted by this crisis we must search for new purpose and meaning in life, seek a long-suffering love, yearn for integrity, and pray for wholeness of personality. This quest finds ultimate direction in the person of Jesus Christ; in relationship to Him one discovers a new quality of life.

The faith for our secular world must be vital and dynamic, communicating God's enduring love and His passion for justice. Such a faith is essential if our values are to be rightly reordered and our gifts properly used—both as individuals and a nation. As the gravity of our challenges increases each day, the need for this reconciling faith becomes more urgent.

We must begin by grasping the true nature of life when it is focused on Christ. In the following pages Myron Augsburger explores the dimensions of this life with refreshing and creative perspectives. Dr. Augsburger presents ideas and insights which can guide us in a growing knowledge of the One who is Life.

Mark O. Hatfield
United States Senator

FAITH
FOR A
SECULAR WORLD

1

*While many ask, "How can one be-
lieve?" it must also be asked, "How
can one not believe?" Unbelief is even
more difficult than belief. Faith is not
strange to one who faces life honestly.
Saving faith is simply normal faith in
the Saving Person!*

Faith Is Inescapable

Life is so constituted that it must be lived in relationship. Less
than this is less than a full life. In relating to another in fellowship,
it is absolutely essential that we believe in one another. Confidence
is the foundation upon which true friendship rests. Shared love is
the ultimate expression that one is trusted. Christian faith and
Christian love is the ultimate reconciliation between man and
God.

In an ordered universe, witnessing mutely to the intelligence of a designer, it is inconceivable that the Designer should be less than anyone of us as thinking men. To believe, to express faith, is not a blind wish, but it is the extension of the reason and awareness within one's self. One who does not believe in God, who stops short of faith in an intelligent personality infusing life with purpose, has the greater problem. He must give a definite answer for his own position.

There are those who call for proof, forgetting that some things in life transcend proof. They are accepted as "given," or are known only in the category of faith. One may not have seen his paternal grandparents, yet he needs no proof. A wife or husband cannot "prove" that their companion loves them even though they have much evidence! God is Person, and one does not prove Him as an "it," as an object of investigation. God is His own proof, one must come to Him in faith.

Should one affirm that he cannot believe in God without proof, he is operating on a basis that he will not apply in other inter-personal areas of relationship. In fact, if in a denial of faith one should deny God, even this denial is a faith position! One cannot prove scientifically that there is no God—thus to affirm this is to take a stance of faith. To believe that there is a God is a faith stance, as it cannot be scientifically proven. But this stance of faith can be evidenced in the lives of thousands as bringing mean-ing into life. That there is evidence against faith in our world no thinking person questions, but there is also evidence of faith.

The sixteenth century saw a new discovery of existential faith in Christ. But the tendency of man is away from faith. He seeks relation to structures of doctrine and reason that he can view as his achieved security, and so by the seventeenth century men had made a god out of dogma, by the eighteenth century they made a god out of reason, by the nineteenth century the god was man, and in the twentieth century we've made a god of scientific achievement. But even now we are recognizing that it takes more than technology to provide man with meaning and values in life. Faith is an inescapable necessity.

Before one can reject faith and be at ease, he must answer the dilemma of non-faith. It is harder to live in our world and not believe in God. Faith is a venture, not an escape, it is risking all on Christ, not an argument. Of our tendency to cover our refusal to acknowledge God by the claim of intellectual problems Eleanor Slater says:

> Though you be scholarly, beware
> The bigotry of doubt.
> Some people take a strange delight
> In blowing candles out.[1]

To reject God is to confine one's life within the narrow walls of the self. Secularism is as old as man himself; it is the attempt to order life without God. It is said that Professor Adler left a discussion at a tea quite disgusted, slamming the door after him. One person remarked, "Well, he's gone," to which the hostess replied, "No, that's a closet!" This is man's plight when he attempts to rush from God's presence.

Each of us must ask ourselves several very personal questions. First, do I really believe? That is to say, we must discover whether life is determined by conscious decisions in faith or whether it is capricious. Second, we msut ask if what we believe is really true? Is it true in and of itself? Truth is greater than any man. We must be certain that what we live by is Truth. And third, we must ask ourselves if our faith is a wholesome influence? There is joy in quality living, a joy which reaches beyond the sense of responsibility. Let us be honest about life and its meanings as we live it.

---

[1] James Dalton, ed. *Masterpieces of Religious Verse* (New York: Harper and Row, Publishers, 1948), p. 428.

The proof of life is not in intellectual theories as much as in the satisfying meanings of existence. Jesus said, "I am come that ye might have life, and that more abundantly."

The question of life is not simply what do you think about God, but how do you feel about God? That is, do you want God in your life? Faith or trust is basically a matter of the will. In today's conversation in higher education there is often an assumption that the cynic is more honest than the committed person. But, this disregards the fact that cynicism is irresponsible with respect to the constructive aspects of life. Furthermore, the cynic is dishonest with respect to the larger dimensions of knowledge and his denial of the spirit of inquiry in such areas. This is illustrated in the story of the college student whose faith was being belittled by his professor. Following numerous lengthy discussions and impressed by the professor's learning, he asked, "What percent of the world's knowledge do you think you understand?" The professor thought a moment and then answered, "I suppose about three percent." The young fellow's next question was, "Has it occurred to you that God might be in the other ninety-seven percent?"

The Christian faith is not contrary to reason, it is reasonable; it simple affirms that God is not found by reason alone. Reason and faith move hand-in-hand in the learning experience. The Christian affirms by faith that God has acted in history to reveal Himself, that there is meaning in history because God is acting through it, that history does not contain its own fulfillment within itself, that God has an ultimate purpose for history as it comes to its focus in His presence. Man, child of the dust and child of God, is made for two worlds. We enjoy the full meaning of life in this one as the reality of the ultimate world overlaps the present.

Faith is not difficult, God in grace makes it the gift of gifts. You can trust God if you but hear Him. In giving Him audience you will share the awesome experience of identity with the Creator.

2

Religion is man's search for God—but Christian faith sees God laying hold on man! For those who think belief in God is only a projection of a father-fixation, perhaps unbelief in God is a projection of father hatred! But for those who know God in fellowship, the experience of faith is the sharing of life with Him. Christ is not one among many! He is the full and final disclosure of God. The salvation He offers is reconciliation with God and with one's fellows.

True Religion Is Not A Crutch

Shall we affirm that religion is for the weakling, that the strong do not need it? No, for Christian faith is not a religion that one uses. Faith is relation with the Person from above, the One who has laid hold on us. If you can live your faith it is too small! To live in a world where Christ is risen is to be called to a quality of life greater than our own capacities.

Christian religion is not a tool with which one can "shore up" his own weakness. It is involvement with Jesus Christ. Like being in love, it must be experienced to be understood. And it is never experienced fully apart from relation to a Person. One in love marries to share life, not as a crutch to meet some selfish need. Accepting Christ as Lord in one's life, yielding one's self to Him as a disciple, is wholly other than seeking to use Him for one's own ends.

Religion is not real for many people primarily because they don't consider it important. Take a look at yourself. Whatever commands your attention most is the thing that counts most with you. Your true religion is that which lies at the heart of your life. This is why the Christian faith calls for a complete reorientation of life. When the center of control in one's life passes from self to Christ, he has truly been born again.

This relationship moves a person beyond religion, beyond something that we have—to Someone who has us! We move beyond forms to fellowship, sharing the total life with Christ. We move beyond duty to devotion, motivated from within rather than by a constraint imposed on a legal basis. We move beyond piety to participation in the work of Christ. Discipleship is to share His mission, not to satiate one's emotional needs by subjective sublimations. God is not so interested in meeting our emotional hungers as He is in transforming us for effective living.

But this is not to say that we do not need God. That would be sheer idolatry. No man is completely a self by himself! This is true in all of life. We need God if we are to know wholeness of life, even as we need friends if we are to enjoy friendship. But to need another person in relationship calls us to a sharing of mutual satisfaction rather than one using the other. This is the meaning of the expression in the Westminster Catechism—"Man's chief end is to glorify God and to enjoy Him forever."

Faith is an attitude in relation to God, a sharing of one's life with Him. Faith is not an escape from problems; it is facing the problem with God! Nor is it as the little boy thought when he saw his grandmother reading her Bible and called, "Look, Granny is cramming for her finals." Faith is something you live by. It is the awareness that life is bigger than yourself. Your choice of sharing life with God makes you bigger than your ego.

Such faith converts; it changes the course of direction in one's life. It transforms the inner man. Here the deepest psychological aspects of life are affected by this basic change at the center of a life. All of life is changed, for now there is a new identification, a new direction and a new motivation.

The focus of New Testament faith is the resurrection of Jesus Christ. Our faith-involvement with Him is a relational experience which makes life new. Entering into relationship with another person involves not only an awareness of them but a new awareness of yourself! In relation to the Christ, this awareness calls you to a new level of being through His greatness and influence upon your life. The key to this transformation is surrender to Him. Under His Lordship the surrendered life is reborn. While this is experienced in the moment of faith, we recognize that faith is an attitude which keeps this relation abreast of our development. As one has said, "I yield as much of myself as I understand today to as much of Christ as I understand today!"

But resurrection is not simply event, it is power—the power to transcend the death dealing influence of sin. This is at one and the same time power to be free from the slavery of sin in life and power to escape the ultimate estrangement from God in death. Being "baptized into Christ," we participate in the meaning of His death (in our surrender of the sinful way of life) and share the power of His resurrection (in a new level of life). The Church of Christ is a community of the resurrected, a community of the Spirit Who quickens our mortal beings now, a community of freedom for life at its highest level.

Faith is no crutch—it is a creative power because it shares the freedom of the risen Christ. Consequently, the Church is not simply a social gathering but a brotherhood of quickened persons, continuing the extension of the resurrection power through the bondage of time. It is not simply the knowledge of God which the Church passes on but the transcendent power of God to be new men and women! We are a continuation of the resurrection more than a "continuation of the incarnation."

❧ 3 ❧

Holiness is wholeness—
  it means that one belongs
  completely to God, that
  one is completely His.
Holiness as wholeness
  means completeness of life,
  the restoration into fellowship with
    God,
  the restoration of the "imago Dei."
Holiness is grace transforming us
whole,
  faith which permits God to be Him-
    self in us!

Whole Persons

One is truly a man made in God's image only as he comes to full self-awareness in the grace of God. The quest for identity continually raises the question, "Am I a self, or am I simply the projection of the will and decisions of others?" But, as this question is pursued, we become aware that we are not all that we have the capacity to become. The awareness of the infinite, of the realm of the eternal, in turn awakens the anxiety of our own finitude. We know we're going to die, and we worry about it.

Step by step our world is tying itself in knots. There is no human solution to our dilemma. We know that the full potential of life will not be engaged in our brief years! Life is more than a matter of time, however, it is a matter of quality.

Man without fellowship with God is not a complete man. Just as man was created for community, for fellowship, and is not complete in isolation, so man is not complete without God. Man is spirit being, and estranged from God his spirit function is incomplete. As a consequence, his psychical nature is without its monitor and runs rampant in selfishness; his physical nature lacks the spirit dynamic and sinks to lower levels of lust and the dominance of fleshly appetites. Honest man cries out, "Oh wretched man that I am, who shall deliver me from the body of this death?"

Wholeness begins with a true sense of self-identity. Actually, one only discovers his real self when confronted with Christ. In Jesus Christ we not only see what God is like, but we also see what true man is like. Confronted by Him, we recognize the perversions in our own lives; we see how far we have turned from the good and noble. The final condemnation of our sinfulness comes from His example. But in grace we discover that while we cannot stand up to Christ, we can stand up with Him! We can make a decision and take a positive stand for Him. We can confess before all the world our identification with Him as Lord. Believing that God has acted uniquely in Christ, this has implications for the whole of life.

To come under the authority or Lordship of Christ is to free one for the larger life! There is no one so much a slave as the person who has had his own way all his life. The one who lives under his own authority has a life no larger than himself. One who lives under the authority of Christ has his life expanded to include all that Christ offers. And at the deepest level we believe that to which we give allegiance.

Wholeness is possible only through identification with ultimate purpose. In a faith-relation with Christ our lives share the meaning of integrity and love, aspects of a whole life that are mutually inclusive. In sharing God's compassion or love we share His conviction of right. Reject Him, and T. S. Elliot asks:

> Where is the life we have lost in living?
> Where is the wisdom we have lost in knowledge?
> Where is the knowledge we have lost in information?
> The cycle of heaven in twenty centuries
> Bring us farther from God and nearer to the Dust.[1]

A modern world claims that it has come of age. Man has grown up! God is said to have entered the world in Christ as man, died, and left the world to man. Now many believe we are experiencing the absence of God! But many of us ask, where is the evidence that man has come of age, that man can live responsibly without God? Again, many of us affirm that God is quite alive, that we know Him, and that He does transform and bring meaning to life. And we have found this true in experience. He does make life new even today in our secular age. In the wholeness He brings, we are able to serve a fragmented world.

Wholeness or holiness comes through the superiority of the spirit in the human personality. The expression, "Holiness is health," is true when the civil war within has ended by an experience of holiness, meaning that one is completely God's possession. Holiness is wholeness, for it involves the total unitary being of the believer. This is not a pietistic subjectivism, but it is a transforming relation with the Sovereign Spirit. It is not the rejection of a part of one's being, even the erotic, but it is the permeation of the total person including the erotic by the *agape* of the Spirit. This whole-

---

[1]James Dalton, ed. *Masterpieces of Religious Verse* (New York: Harper and Row, Publishers, 1948), p. 491.

ness rejects the dualism of soul and body in an experience of grace in which man's sin-shattered spirit is reborn. In addition, Christ gives one the Holy Spirit to indwell and to transform. In the new synthesis of soul and body, one has an answer for the neuroses so common in modern man. Neurosis is a cry for help when the natural soul is repressed rather than regenerated! When repressed, it cannot breathe, or live since it is excluded from the freedom of spiritual integration.

There is a transparent honesty called for if we are to achieve wholeness. The Spirit will help us "strip the soul" in an experience of spiritual hygiene, until the lower levels of the soul are refined and revitalized. Apart from this deeper penetration of the Spirit, we will suffer a spiritual atrophy. When the inner man, the real you, does not live honestly with its own understanding, it cannot live in clear perception of God. The condition of spiritual health has a definite bearing on the perception of our minds and senses. Opening the life to God's truth involves one's whole being in the transformation of His grace.

Ever since the Apostle Paul, men have thought of the transforming experience of grace through involvement in faith, hope, and love. Faith is the attitude which thinks with Christ. This mental communion liberates us from fear and engages us in complete trust in one whom we have not seen. This "leap of faith" is totally other than man's basic tendency to trust only that which he can master and prove. The person who can trust no one is admitting that he is insecure. Fear is a basic insecurity, a desire to be master in every situation, and a frustration that life is too large for this to be our lot! Faith answers this by trusting ourselves totally to the ultimate Master.

Hope is even more illusive, for in hope we participate in the purpose of Christ's life—a further progress of faith, an awakening within our souls by the announcement of a future event. The full and final purpose of God influences us in the present. This is the transforming power of the "last things" of which John writes, "Every man that has this hope in Him purifies himself even as He is pure."

In love we open our total life to another person, to a Thou. In this experience the personality is truly alive. Love draws us beyond ourselves in a manner which expands and enriches, transforming the self. Love only flourishes as life is viewed from the perspective of the loved one! In this way love for God reorients life, *agape* sanctifies *eros,* as the energy of divine love penetrates the whole of life. In this relation, we share the essence of Christianity—a personal relation between God and the believer. In this reconciliation man is completed, he is healed, and finds the shattered character of his self enjoying wholeness through the synthesis brought by the Spirit.

ɞ **4** ɞ

As one cannot see himself without a mirror, so one cannot fully understand himself without another. As moderns, the understanding of ourselves is conditioned by our society . . . a society of anomi (the loss of a norm), of anonymity (the loss of identity), and of anomosity (the loss of the joy of friendship). How does one build a life of character in the fragmented world of today? Can we, unless we know One who understands us completely?

Understanding One's Self

Confronted with the need of understanding one's self, you may be saying, "I wish I could." And you are right. The last person in the world that you will fully understand is yourself! And yet we affirm, "God understands us." This is the marvel of divine grace! God understands us in our perversion and yet graciously shares Himself with us. In His Word, in His action in human history, we meet ourselves again and again, and in His analysis we begin to understand ourselves. In relation to Him, we understand our freedom and our sin, we find that men may be stubborn enough to say "no" to God forever.

If we would achieve wholeness, we must admit our inner problems. But God isn't simply dealing with problems we have, He is dealing with the problem we are! One little fellow remarked, "I have something inside of me that I can't do what I want to with." If we would understand ourselves, we must begin with the recognition of our self-centeredness. It is from this that we need to be saved, now! God's grace calls us to newness of life—a life which He shares in love, in reconciliation with Himself. The only deliverance from being self-oriented is to become other-oriented, Christ-oriented. This is the new birth, the new beginning, a birth from above.

Most illusive in this understanding of one's self is the matter of motive. The question is not as much "what you do," but "why you do what you do." More important than what you do is the spirit that possesses or motivates you—this is the measure of life. In Jesus' "Sermon on the Mount," He continually points us to the question of motive. This is the greatest "deeper-life" sermon Jesus preached. Even in good things, one may do what is right in a wrong spirit. The result to one's self is wrong, good though the work may be, for it is not a work of faith.

The greatest crisis of life is in one's own spirit. We find it easy to defend the self and blame the other, as the little fellow who said, "It all started when Jimmy hit me back." To face one's self honestly, to confess one's rejection of (or use of) others as sin, is a major step toward victory. From what source do our social ills arise if it is not from the selfishness that uses others for personal gain, that rejects people or races for the supposed security of one's own, that manipulates others for the satisfaction of power? Jesus said the meek shall inherit the earth. They alone shall know how to enjoy to the full its true worth!

To be a real self one must live in relation with others, and above all, with God. This is a relationship, an experience of communion with another. As Tournier says, "Information is intellectual, whereas communion is spiritual; . . . information speaks of personages. Communion touches persons."[1] It is in communion that we share our real selves. In relating to others, rather than using them, we discover what we are like ourselves.

Many persons are looking for life, for the ability to live a real, authentic life. The quest will never be satisfied short of honesty. Once we learn to be honest with ourselves, transparent before God, and open with our fellows, we will discover the joy of being a true self. Having thus found the way to overcome self-deception we are ready to become participants in creative living. The question is, how can one become what he ought to be? How can one actualize his potential? Each person has particular endowments which can be actualized to the full in the grace of God. We overcome frustration by seeing our role as one part of a larger purpose and program. We overcome envy when we accept God's right to assign each his role in life. We overcome aggression when we recognize that our complete fulfillment is never at the expense of another.

The person who is reconciled to God has found in the experience of honest confession and humble repentance the way to be reconciled to his fellowmen. Conversion gives one a new potential by the indwelling Spirit. By the integrative processes of faith, this potential is to be actualized in personality integration, in social responsibility, in the expression of love in Christian service. The measure of the true size of one's self is in the size of that to which we give our allegiance.

Today, when men react against authoritarian forms of religion,

---

[1]Paul Tournier, *The Meaning of Persons* (New York: Harper and Row, Inc., 1957), p. 25.

there is need for individual religious experience. The gifts of the Spirit are in recognition of the fact that each person is unique and each is different, and yet together, we make up the body of Christ. The unity of the Christian brotherhood is at a higher level than a structured uniformity. The larger unity of spirit and cause provides freedom for the development of each individual's potential. In the New Testament we read that the disciples understood the meaning of Christ's message while it was hidden to others. This is what makes us disciples—understanding the inner meaning of the Gospel. Concerning others, our Lord said simply, "Let the dead bury the dead"; let those who live only for that which is passing take care of the passing!

౨ 5 ౨

Man is a unitary being,
Life should not be a civil war within—
Our health depends on inner harmony,
Our souls being not fragmented, but
* whole.*
To live in sin is to live for self,
For life to be centered in one's ego:
But the change comes in being Chris-
* tians,*
In life being centered in Christ,
In Him all things cohere in balance;
In Christ man is a unit.

Christ, the Center of Life

If your life is to find its meaning from what stands at its center, you must exercise the greatest care in choosing that center. What "thing," what "it," is great enough to build your life around? Will you measure the center of your life in dollars and cents? Will you wrap yourself around your own appetites to be governed and shaped by them? Will you move your spirit into the periphera and place lust at the heart of your life? Is popularity to be regarded as more important than real personhood? Your life is too important to build it around anything or anyone less than Christ!

The fact of the Christ event is an indelible part of history. There is a "happenedness" about the work of Christ in history which cannot be erased. All honest minds must reckon with the fact of His life and message. Believing in the supreme value of personality, here is one Personality we cannot ignore. His claims must be faced, either in belief or nonbelief. For those who stay in nonbelief, there is the inescapable fact that He outlined a philosophy of life superior to any other. For those who believe that God was in Christ, there is an inescapable mandate to tell all men! In fact, evangelism is the Church expressing her true nature in action. It is organizing life with Christ at the center.

But Christ at the center? How do you achieve this? He isn't here in form, so what now—Is He idea, mystical sensation, or a legalistic example? This problem is resolved when you recognize that life has a truly spiritual dimension. This Christ is a living Person whose spiritual presence is as real as thought or love. To meet Him in His Word is to know about Him, but to open your spirit to Him is to know Him as Lord in your life. Day by day, you can acknowledge both His presence and His leading. This means conscious awareness of belonging to Him. From Him, you gain your principles of direction and the power to implement them.

Deep within the heart of every person something or someone wears a crown. Each individual decides what or whom he is going to worship. Our way of life expresses our loyalties, as the balance of a wheel gives evidence as to whether it is on center. A person expresses in life whatever he is truly experiencing within himself. When our lives fail to express the righteousness of grace, we must discover the inner "rightness" of experiencing His gracious presence and direction.

The believer becomes a member of an association, of Christ's

team. In football the fullback doesn't win the game alone. A choir
member is rarely a good soloist. Life is made up of teamwork.
The astronauts could never make their flights without scores of
others on the team. And yet, when our team wins the game, we
cry, *"We've* won!" And so with the Christian, as a member of
Christ's team—we've won, at Calvary, at the tomb, in life!

Imagine getting into the ring with a professional boxer. In a
few minutes you might be flat on the mat, out for the count.
When you come to and exclaim, "That fellow can really punch,"
you really don't know what you are talking about. But, if you
stay in that ring fifteen rounds and take all that he can hurl into
your body, you can honestly say, "He can really punch." Now,
you know what you are talking about! When we stepped into the
arena with Satan, we were out at the first blow. But Christ
stepped into the arena and took all he could hurl into Him, all
the way to the cross—and never cracked once! Christ alone
knows the full force of temptation. Now we can be on Christ's
team, victors over Satan. In and by the presence of Christ, we
can have victory. "We are more than conquerors through Him
that loved us."

This is an experience of faith, of trusting Him to make His
presence understood. Faith, you should remember, is the attitude
which permits God to be Himself in your life. And you can experience this. He says, "If any man hear my voice and open the
door, I will come in and sup with Him and he with me." You
can't enjoy friendship without accepting another as friend! Begin
conversing with God—you'll find that He has something to say
to you.

What He says is heard ultimately or fully in Jesus Christ. In
Christ, "the Word became flesh and dwelt among us." He expressed the will of God in His total life and person, in what He
said, in what He did and in what He was! In what He said, ex-

pressing the full meaning of the will or law of God. "It has been said . . . . but I say unto you", anything that leads to the sinful act is already a perversion of sin within you! In what He did, for He gave Himself to serve, to teach, to evangelize; He paid taxes, defied political rulers, and served the "church" without "selling out" to the hierarchy. In what He was; no one convinced Him of sin, for He personified Truth, and no one could doubt His love, for He expressed love and forgiveness even to the unlovely in His death. The more we look honestly at Christ the more clear becomes our understanding of God.

When as believers we affirm in faith that "Christ is the answer," we are expressing a deeper truth than most of us understand. Theologically, this means that the key to interpreting life is Christology. He is the center "in whom all things cohere," but He is also the center for interpretation. The message of Holy Scripture unfolds toward Him, and we only understand it when we see the progress in God's disclosure of Himself. He is the full expression of God and His will, consequently, we relate ethics to Christology in the same way that we relate salvation to Christology—both are relational. He is our norm, our absolute, in a world where men are seeing everything as relative and where ethics are described as situational. The decision and the application is situational, to be sure, but the Christian brings His Christology into the situation as the norm. Most advocates of a situational ethic would bring love (agape) into the situation as their norm, but love apart from a higher frame of reference will not remain *agape*. Love receives its true character from the holiness or wholeness of God. Only Christ offers this larger dimension for situational decision, situational communication, and for situational interpretation.

What does a Christological approach to religious life really mean? First, it means placing personalism above moralism, recognizing that only persons are "ends," and codes or laws are only "means" toward ends. Our mission is one of reconciling persons to God and their fellows and to expose and oppose social injustice. Second, Christology places transforming grace above sacramentalism, for in Him we become new creatures, not in the sacrament. The sacrament is only the symbol through which we witness to our new life; the newness is the post-forgiveness relation with the forgiving One. (Post-forgiveness in terms of the new relation entered! Not "post" if you think only moralistically, for there will continue to be pardons.) Third, Christology means that loyalty to the Kingdom of heaven supersedes loyalty to any earthly power. The true Christian is transnational, calling for a spiritual church but a secular government, reminding the government that it is to be modest and fair and to avoid reaching into the realm of religion by decree! There are times that the follower of Christ will still need to say of heads of state, "Go tell that fox . . .!" The Christian's life should be expendable only in the spiritual conquest of building His Kingdom. Wherever this faith truly goes, changing lives, men will beat "their swords into plowshares and their spears into pruning hooks." Fourth, Christology means a covenant community in love wherein we know the dynamic of relating to each other through our being in Christ. Bonhoeffer, in *Life Together,* shows the supreme value of Christian community in that by relating through Christ each is free, neither is coerced, manipulated, or dominated! This is a strategy to create a new humanity in grace. Finally, Christology means a perspective of history which sees God's purpose at work in the world, making men aware that "the Kingdom of God is come near" in anticipation of His Kingdom beyond time, trans-earthy, trans-time, and trans-millennial. In this faith, we live with the ultimate meaning transforming and guiding us in the present. We live now "after the power of an endless life."

While many reject Christianity, it is often not a rejection of Christ as much as a rejection of the perverted picture of Christ which they have received. To affirm that Christ is the answer and then only to raise questions, is blasphemy. Our mission is to take Christ seriously! To be honest about our faith and responsible in its expression in all of life. Sharing His power in "newness of life," we become expressions of the resurrection.

∾ 6 ∾

Freedom is not "from" as much as
"to,"
  Not everyone has freedom,
    To play the piano,
    To sing,
    To love truly, or
    To be whole persons.
  God gives us freedom "to be-
    come! . . ."

Freedom and Obedience

God created man free, but man's own perversion has limited that freedom. Man's sin, his ego-centeredness, limits his freedom. He longs to be free and is frustrated by his bondage. Someone has said, "Inside of every fat man is a thin man trying to get out." Just so, man's true self, his free self, is confined within the strangle hold of his own ego.

To such a man, Christ comes and calls for a response, a decision to follow, to move out of himself into the freedom Christ

offers. Freedom means the privilege of choice through release
from limitations imposed on the self. This is freedom in obedience,
paradoxical as it may be at first seem. We are freed for responsible living. But we are free to say "no" to God. This is the risk
of freedom; God's terrible permission for man to say "no" to his
own destruction.

A selfish heart creates its own vacuum!

Christ's Lordship enlarges; it does not stifle freedom.

His presence overcomes the tendency to withdraw.

As the pendulum of a clock is free to swing so long as it is
attached, so man is free in obedience to God. Jesus said, "Ye shall
know the truth and the truth shall make you free." Again He
said: "If the Son shall make you free, ye shall be free indeed."
This is the freedom to become what God purposes for one.

True freedom is not removal of restraint; this would be license.
Freedom is the power to achieve. Note this carefully—freedom is
not that no one prevents you from playing the piano, freedom
is in being able to play it. It is God who enables us to become all
that He purposes. Kierkegaard said, "God indicates that everything is possible."

For men, this is newness of life, a life under the sovereign will
of Christ. The Christian faith does not put liberation at the
center, but reconciliation, the freedom to live in responsible
relation with another. In grace, one sees freedom and obedience
in direct relationship, for one is free to become in the degree to
which he obeys the call to righteousness in life (John 1:12).

Our non-freedom is due to "the law of sin and death," the law
of ego-centeredness which dominates us. But this law can be overcome by "the law of the spirit of life in Christ Jesus" (Romans
8:2). We can be freed in Him from spurious motives, racial and
class distinctions, slavery to the sensual, and from the idolatry of
materialism. The lack of this "freedom to become" perverts free-

dom into irresponsibility. The consequence is expressed in our fear that the technically able man may blow us all up!

In the freedom of grace, we are called to share the righteousness to which the law could only point. This "rightness" with God is known in Christ, and we now stand in right relation with God in Him. We have not lived rightly, but we are now His in "rightness." If you would ask me whether I am a husband, the answer is, "yes, I am." But if you ask, "Are you a perfect husband?" the answer is "no." I have higher ideals than I've reached. When the question of faith is asked, I respond, "Yes, I belong to Christ, even though I have higher ideals than I've reached." The character of Christianity affirms a higher ideal, even while one confesses he has yet to reach it. This is not hypocrisy; it is the honest facing of failings.

These two, freedom and obedience, belong together. The difference between a river and a swamp is that the river has borders, the swamp has none. The great life, the free life, has borders, it is disciplined and effective. We live in the freedom of obedience. Today, there is a short supply of the credible act. We must share the meaning of obedience if we are to know the freedom of His Spirit. God's law, His will, is always conditioned by His love. There is love in law, as any good parent knows. And there is law in love, as any spouse knows. God, in His sovereignty, is a Being with absolute personal discipline. He calls us to share this discipline for our own wholeness.

Christian freedom enables us to express valid concerns about non-freedom, about social injustice. Anything which destroys persons, or the essence of personhood in individuals or groups of persons, must be changed. The Christian perspective holds social evil and personal evil together because it sees the individual as having ultimate or infinite worth. Communism, by way of contrast, sees the individual as worthless. As Christians, we oppose

injustice—that which robs anyone of the privilege of the fulfillment of his essential personhood. We must answer the problems
of affluence over poverty, of race over race, of ethnic group over
ethnic group. We oppose immorality—that which perverts any
valid role of life for selfish usage in interference with achievement of one's own or another's essential personhood. We oppose
intemperance—that which submits the self to artificial props and
practices which master the person and result in the deterioration
of and destroys the freedom of persons.

But Christian freedom is not a negation of perversions; it is
freedom to be! We are freed for action at the level of influence
for the good. Here we are to transcend the danger of letting the
sub-Christian world determine the structures of our action. We
avoid the danger of simply duplicating a humanistic level of
action, good though it is in a society where the concept of man
has been Christianized to a degree. Our freedom is an action in
grace, expressed by persons unashamedly Christian, using the
realms of the secular as the sphere for Christian influence. We
communicate by example—the result of participating in His
reconciling grace ourselves. In fact, holiness is only transmitted by
example.

7

Peace is "the answer of a good conscience toward God," disciplined, for it refuses to compromise, and enriched, for it is subject to the higher law of God. The man "under authority" has his privileges and his potential increased by the size and character of that authority. A conscience conditioned by the greater will of God makes a man a better person.

Educating the Conscience

Every man, we say, is a free moral agent. This means that each person has powers of choice which determine his character and destiny. While certain factors of both heredity and environment condition those choices, the New Testament places upon us personal responsibility for our choices. And while much of life is determined, man can yet choose. Man has the power to think, and in this process, he can analyze and see opportunity of change. However, this is limited by our sin. The real freedom to choose comes in grace, for when Christ invades our little closed systems of life, He introduces a live option transcending our limitations.

Within man's mind there is a mysterious faculty called conscience. It serves as a tribunal of the soul, passing judgment upon our actions. This conscience speaks on the basis of one's past learning and experience; consequently, what men's consciences say is often quite different. But there is one universal characteristic—regardless of the differences between what men think to be right or wrong—conscience casts its vote on the side of what is thought to be right. This is the universal moral agency, reminding thinking man that he has a moral obligation to follow what he believes to be right. Such a sense of "rightness" directs man to the contemplation of an ultimate "right." Immanuel Kant, the philosopher, developed his system of ethics on the sense of "oughtness." But a God who only answers our sense of moral obligation is less than the God of grace known through Jesus Christ.

The differences between conscience is not to be taken lightly. No one's conscience is to be idolized and followed in the place of God's Word! The Word of God is the standard; the conscience is to be standardized, or educated, by the Word. Differences of conviction should lead us to study the Scripture and seek the mind of the Spirit. It is in the Word that we find direction. Actually, the conscience cannot add new insight of itself. It can only speak in judgment, in harmony with its conditioning. New insight is found in God's revelation, in processes of reason, and in interchange with others.

Many persons are plagued by an overly sensitive conscience. This is often because they have idolized the conscience and set its voice above the voice of Scripture. The conscience is not to be repressed; it is to be reinformed. It is to be enthroned; it is to be educated. When one's convictions are harmonized with the

Word, there is inner direction for righteous living. When one has convictions from his cultural conditioning contrary to the Word, he must honor the Word of God and speak back to his conscience. The conscience will adjust to its education.

But the conscience is a most important guide. It serves as a balance within man's soul. It helps to keep us on course. As such, it is a valuable part of man's personality and should be handled honestly. A person should take seriously the matter of educating his conscience in the Word so that it can speak in harmony with God's will. Our positive guidance comes from His Word and Spirit. Conditioned by these, the more negative conditions or warnings of conscience help keep us in the better way. The honest Christian will seek a conscience "bound by the Holy Spirit."

Happy is the man whose conscience has been laid hold on by God, educated in His truth, and who then obeys in "good conscience toward God." The amazing thing about the Christian Church is that while claiming to live under the Lordship of Christ, so often the consciences of the members are conditioned more by their particular culture or religious tradition than by the Word of God. Many evangelical Christians have strong conviction on minutia but little conscience on major matters of faith. Jesus said of minutia, "These ought ye to have done, but not to leave the other undone" . . . justice, mercy and love. While it is good to have a conscience on smoking and resulting lung cancer, we need to have our consciences sharpened on the evils of inequality for the races, on war and mass killing, on materialism and enforced poverty on the many, for the privileges gained by the few. Many people look to the Church for a word from the Lord and all they hear is "the echo of their own voice." Often they reject Christ without hearing Him. Perhaps, it is more accurate to say that they reject the perverted picture of Christ which they receive more than they reject Him.

Our secular world has shoved God from the center and placed man there. Now modern man finds it difficult to even think "God." This humanism needs to be met with the more daring humanism expressed by Paul at Mars' Hill. There is a true Man to stand at the center of life and interpret it—the God-man, Jesus Christ. In Him "the Word became flesh and dwelt among us." In Him the full essence of humanity is expressed while at the same time we see in Him the true essence of God. Confronting man in his lostness, "on the borderline of the human situation," in His death and resurrection, He brings us to a new level of faith. Now, in the midst of dread we can say "yes" to Him. By this identification we then find meaning for all of life. Committed to Christ as Lord, our consciences are both educated in and bound by His example and will.

∾ 8 ∾

Man's basic sin is the idolizing of self. We express our pride in either status that lords it over others or in sensuality that uses others. The true purpose for life is found in the will of God. In His will we find the greatest possible fulfillment in life.

Accepting God's Will

Through the centuries and around the world Christians have uttered as basic the creed, "Christ is Lord." At the same time we have expressed our sin by affirming our own lordship, failing to serve Him. Christ is actually not our Lord until we are His servants. Until we surrender our will to His will, the tension remains between us. Psychologically, surrender is the heart of conversion. This surrender is the cost of grace. As Dietrich Bonhoeffer makes clear, when Jesus calls a man, He does not call him to come and dine but to come and die.[1]

---

[1]Dietrich Bonhoeffer, *The Cost of Discipleship* (New York: The Macmillan Company, 1951), p. 73.

There is a divine will for man—the question is, are we ready to accept it? This is the crucial issue—do we want to do God's will? Faith is not a matter of the mind as much as of the will. This means that our spiritual experience is first a matter of our wills. It is good to ask one's self, "How do I feel about God? Do I want to share my life with God?" Jesus said, "If any man wills to do His will, he shall know of the doctrine." In a real sense the disciple is one who says, "I obey in order to understand." While this is contrary to the rational pattern we outline, it is actually the test of our accepting His Lordship.

Abraham went—not knowing where, but he obeyed.

Joseph obeyed—not knowing the outcome nor having promise of the future.

Moses made a decision and acted, knowing not what lay before, only that his faith called him to act.

Our Lord again and again placed himself in the hands of the Father in acts of trust, leaving all to Him.

Many have written on how to find God's will; the question here is accepting it. One of the signs of spiritual maturity is patience, respecting God's right to work out plans beyond our understanding and serving Him in trust. He is Lord of the universe, you can trust Him and accept His will for you. Refuse to accept His right to assign your role in life and you are guilty of treason against your better self. This is the chief test of one's commitment —obedience to the will of God.

What is your faith—really? Are you His subject? Are you discovering how to recognize the sovereign will of the Spirit? There is joy in the yielded life, plus the stimulus to achieve where He has assigned you. Begin by answering the issue of wanting His will. Then study the principles by which Christ lived until they become your guide in decision making. Beware of expecting divine leading apart from the hard work of thinking through the implications of an issue. Pray honestly for the leading of the Spirit. Test your conclusions by discussion with spiritual minded persons. Now move in faith and give God His opportunity to confirm the leading. Each day becomes an exciting new experience as you share with Him in discoveries of life.

The yielded life is not a surrender of active participation; it is the surrender of autonomy so that one can participate in His greater good. Modern man is autonomous man, but he doesn't know what to do with his autonomy. To seek God's will is to harmonize one's life with His values. God's will for character is universal; He purposes wholeness for all of us. But His will for service is individual, a design and a responsibility that fits each particular case. This is first a matter of purpose, the program and place are secondary. A given life finds its greatest joy in fulfilling the purpose for which God designed it. A personal friend, Bishop John L. Stauffer, once said, "As I look back over my life, if I had it to live over, I'd make the same basic decisions." He was satisfied that he had honestly sought God's will.

In a secular age men tend to regard history as containing its own fulfillment. Serious minded men seek to find direction from the human situation alone. We need a new awareness of divine purpose transcending the human predicament. Mankind continues to tie history into knots, but the strand of divine purpose is still there. In the midst of human despair the believing heart still lives in hope. And by this hope we are saved—saved from dread, futility, meaningless, and the loss of our true being. We can affirm life in the midst of a dying age as we share the power of the resurrection.

~ 9 ~

"Our Father in heaven,
We hallow Thy name;

May Thy Kingdom holy,
On earth be the same;

Give to us daily,
Our portion of bread;

For 'tis from Thy bounty,
That all must be fed;

Forgive our transgressions,
And keep us from sin;

For Thine is the Kingdom,
Forever — Amen."

(Author of Paraphrase unknown)

Prayer that Counts

Most people pray even though some do not recognize it as such. It is simply the cry of helplessness. This is at least an awareness that life is larger than ourselves. Others pray in genuine conversation with God, knowing that they share with Him in the program of the ages.

God is at work in this world, but in ways consistent with His holiness and His integrity. He respects the dignity and freedom of humanity even though man has sinned. Prayer is not a magic force which overrides man's own choices. It is a miracle of association by which one can identify himself with God in the midst of a perverted age.

Prayer is not overcoming God's reluctance to act; it is opening one's life to God's willingness. Prayer is giving God the moral freedom to move in areas where He has wanted to but waited out of respect for the freedom of man. Often, He is waiting for us to invite Him. We can not use prayer to demand God to align the affairs of the world with our perspective. Rather, prayer should bring us into line with God's perspective. This is its strength, transforming us into harmony with God's will, infusing us with the security and assurance that we are participants in life with an eternal quality.

Prayer is first of all *honesty*. A person who participates in life given to him by God but who ignores God is basically dishonest. To live as though one is self-sufficient is treason both against one's higher capacities and against God. Only prayer enables us to actualize spiritual potential.

Prayer is an expression of thankfulness for life and all its pleasures. Believing prayer begins with respect and reverence, "Our Father, which art in heaven." It moves to recognition of His will as better than ours, "Thy will be done on earth as it is in heaven." We acknowledge our absolute dependence upon God for the necessities of life: physically, "Give us this day our daily bread"; spiritually, "Forgive us our debts as we forgive our debtors," and "Lead us not into temptation, but deliver us from evil."

Prayer is humility. Here is the acknowledgement that one is not his own god. In prayer we transcend our own will by identification with the will of the Father. In this conversation with God we express our awareness that each day of life is a gift. And, most significantly, we humbly confess our own guilt and need of forgiveness in a context which applies the attitude of forgiveness to those who have wronged us. There is no arrogance in true prayer, for we confess that we cannot trust ourselves when we ask God to keep us from situations which make sinning easy. The test of one's prayer life is not in time, it is in the spirit of humility which makes prayer as natural as breathing. God moves through common men who pray with a freedom denied to "great" men who will not pray.

Prayer is an expression of hope. Men who pray are not in despair; they touch the hand of the Almighty. The man of prayer is the man of poise. The measure of a man's strength is not so much when he is on his toes as when he is on his knees. Here he tunes his soul to the melody of heaven. Here his vision is set on the majesty of the Eternal. Here his concern for his brother is sanctified by the spirit of Another who "is not ashamed to call us brethren." Hope is the certainty that "He which has begun a good work in you will perform it unto the day of the end." It is the conviction that God not only has acted but is acting in history. And as we face the despair of this age, the decadence of life, and the deterioration of social and international relations, we do not panic, for we live by hope.

Let us accept the direction of the Master in prayer. When He walked among men, He prayed. He believed that He was conversing with a real Person-Being! He affirmed that He was conforming His life to the will of the Father. For man, He leaves with us the words, "Men ought always to pray and not to faint." Do not think of God as far away—out there. Wherever God is, in terms of sphere, it is not a spatial but a spiritual sphere to which we refer. Christian theology has not said He is "out there" or "up there," but rather that He is present everywhere. The term "omnipresent" means that He is here, that He is available for encounter everywhere and at any time. When we pray, "Our

Father which art in heaven," we do not mean One who sits on another planet, but One who is in the heavenly or spiritual realm. When Jesus ascended "to the right hand of God the Father," He went from our physical realm to the spirit realm. In His gift of the Holy Spirit to be with us, God is not far away; He is moved in. Prayer is not magic to get a distant, authoritarian ruler of the universe to do something for our good—He will not be used—it is sharing our lives with Him who shares Himself with us. And at what a cost to Himself! "Your Heavenly Father knoweth what things you have need of before you ask Him." Come in prayer, then, to receive *Him*.

ᴥ **10** *ᴥ*

*The way one relates to others is a true
expression of his character and faith.
To share the inner self is an experience
of faith. Only one who opens his life
fully to Christ knows the joy of
"sharing with" rather than "using"
another.*

Relating to Others Through Christ

Man is created in and for fellowship. No man is complete of himself alone. Our lives are influenced by and enriched in relation to others. But, enriching one another presupposes a meaningful and a sanctified relationship. If the relationship is unholy, the lives tend to degenerate.

Modern man is characterized by a gnawing loneliness which he seeks to escape in the crowd. This loneliness is a condition of inner isolation of an ego-barrier that will not share with others. Paradoxical as it may seem, the true cure for loneliness is to get alone with God, to find one's self at rest in Him. Loneliness is corrected by a sense of belonging.

When one relates to others, it can be either meanly or meaningfully. Often we tend to relate in ways that dominate or manipulate others, in ways which exhibit ego-struggles rather than fellowship, or in attempts at using or possessing another. To relate in true Christian brotherhood is different. It is impossible for a man singly to live in a culture and to maintain views other than those of the culture. To rise above the status quo calls for meaningful relationships with those who will covenant together in faith. In Christian faith one shares with others in and through Christ. Without Christ there is often discord or tension. When you relate through Christ, each is free and yet each shares with satisfaction.

Relating through Christ is to relate in honor, love, and equity. *Honor* is respect for the importance of human personality. Kant expressed this as a categorical imperative, "Treat every person as an end in himself not as a means to an end." *Love* is opening your life to share with others in a manner that is for their good. When you truly love, you open your life to meet needs or enrich the lives of others. And love "covers over" the tendency to a multitude of sins. If you love your neighbor as your self, you will not use him, you will not kill, you will not steal, you will not commit immorality. "Love worketh no ill to its neighbor." *Equity* comes through each "esteeming others better than ourselves," looking out for their well-being, knowing that each answers to God for the opportunities He offers us. Remember, there is often more sin in plenty than in poverty.

The full expression of this principle should be found in Christian community. The term "community" refers to a dynamic of relationship rather than a sociological grouping. The sharing of regenerate people is best expressed as brotherhood. This is a close involvement of persons in common faith, in "community." The dynamic of this sharing is relating through Christ. We find in Him our common ground of relationship and common directive for service. As members together in the Kingdom of Heaven, we share with Christ in the work of reconciliation. In Him we are freed from the tendency to use others, to manipulate, humiliate, coerce, or to dominate. This is a new community which has the potential of changing the world.

Our fragmented society should see in the Christian Church the corrective for our shattered condition. Alienated from God, man finds himself alienated from his fellows. Man needs a sound basis for relating to his fellows. Christianity answers this need in the person of Christ. In His gracious presence, persons can meet in freedom, enrich one another's lives, and share the full purpose of the social interchange. This happens in grace, for Jesus said, "Where two or three are met in my name, there am I in the midst of them." His presence, His Spirit, calls us to higher levels of relation.

The community of believers should function under the authority of Christ and beware of sinking back into the world in social accommodation. When the church accommodates itself economically, socially, or spiritually to the sub-Christian levels of society, it is a "fallen Church." The true Church is free, not structured by either social orders or governments, but by the Lord of heaven. It is established under the direction of the Spirit. Its total membership enters a covenant relation to further work of Christ. Each believer has a personal ministry by reason of his baptismal vows— one of witnessing to the reality of resurrection life. Within the covenant community, sharing in Christ will result in a style of life, in a disciplined community. But the modern church has become an undisciplined assembly. The great Quaker scholar, Rufus Jones said, "The American Churches are like Robinson Crusoe's goat pasture, the fields are so large and the fences so far apart that the goats inside are as wild as the goats without!" Let us rediscover the fellowship of discipline, that we might be truly a company of disciples.

11

I stood at Dachau in the rain,
And it was night
The drops splashed in circles
To widen and disappear
And then be replaced
By others, and still others.

I stood at Dachau, and its night
Dropped around me—
The faces were there without name,
They had come and gone,
Destroyed by the tyranny of man;
To pass and make room for others
Is Dachau a memory, or our fate?

M.S.A.

My Brother's Keeper?

The answer is no! You are not your brother's keeper, as much as there may be times when you might wish you were! Have you wished you could determine someone's course in life for him? Cain behaved this way and found that it led to the destruction of his brother. In self-defense he asked of God, "Am I my brother's keeper?" His question was intended as cover for his violation of his brother's rights. God's answer spans the Bible, interpreting the question, and broadening our understanding of how we relate to others. God did not answer, "Yes, you are," but rather, "the voice of your *brother's* blood cries to me." To "keep" another is to violate his freedom. The desire to rule another is always wrong. Our relationship is of a superior type.

You are not your brother's keeper, you are your brother's brother! This is our Lord's answer. When Jesus told the story of the good Samaritan, the question He presented at the end was not, "Do you see who your neighbor is?" but rather "Are you willing to be neighborly?" We are not called to be judges of our brethren, keepers of their lives. We are called to share, to be brotherly. Humanly, we tend toward being keepers, and if we cannot keep or control someone, we withdraw or perhaps would even destroy them. When we try to be our brother's keeper, we get into difficulty, for this increases our pride and arrogance and in turn tends to destroy his individuality.

Unless our relationships are proper, we are contributing to the continued social ills of our day. Can a Christian speak of race in terms of inequity, describing people as "all right in their place"? Can a happy marriage be had when two persons live in competition and each spouse seeks to control the other rather than live in the freedom of love? Can the generation gap between parents and children be overcome if children fail to honor and parents fail to share in understanding love? Can we truly evangelize if the impression is that we are primarily out to add numbers to our membership rolls? Can we correct the international problems if strong nations act to control or keep "lesser" nations instead of being brotherly to them?

One can neither act in coercion nor in condescension and still be his brother's brother. To coerce, manipulate, or violate the life of another is wrong. On the other hand, to relate in condescension or mere tolerance only breeds hatred. And knowing God's will that we live by love, you cannot hate your brother without hating your brother's God. Remember, each person counts equally with God. In sharing your life with God, you will share it in His way with your brother. This perspective on life will transform your relations with others. As Samuel Shoemaker has said, "There is enough time each day to treat each person you meet as a person!" And this is to be done in loving acceptance, not in mere tolerance!

In Isaiah 41:6 we read, "They helped everyone his neighbor; and every one said to his brother, Be of good courage." This is the strength of Christian brotherhood; our love for and our concern for the wellbeing of others. Being our brother's brother, we will find the way to encourage him in life. Rather than having a competitive spirit, we will recognize each other as team members. Rather than being censorious, we will be helpful. Out of a spirit of concern for our brother, we will share in a positive and enriching fellowship. As we live with this spirit, we will find that "charity covers a multitude of sins;" it prevents our sinning against others.

Love by its nature is active, not passive. Jesus introduced the role of love as a strategy for advancing the Kingdom. The ultimate expression of love is not in giving things but in giving one's self. In the service of Christians this ultimately means winning another to be my brother in Christ. This is the essential aspect of evangelism, winning the estranged to Christ and involving them in the covenant community. Strange as it may seem, since we are all sinners accepted in grace, our greatest limitation in evangelism is our inability to accept others as our brothers in Christ. Unfortunately, we have been working at this matter backwards—always attempting to remake the other. We should concentrate on being brotherly!

12

To forgive is costly, to carry one's own
wrath
On the sin of another;
The guilty one is released,
The offended frees him, by
Bearing his own indignation
And resolving it in love
God forgives by carrying His own
wrath
On the sin we've expressed against
Him;
The depth of our guilt is seen at the
Cross,
The greatness of His love matched it,
for
"He bare our sins in His own body,"
He absorbs our guilt and makes us
free.
Forgiveness goes through the sin to
freedom.

Forgiveness, Not Tolerance

Forgiveness is the most costly thing in the universe. No one truly forgives without paying a price himself for the offense of another. To forgive one who has wronged you means that you free him and literally carry your own indignation on his sin. Carrying your own wrath on the other's offense means that you do not humiliate him. This is what God did at Calvary. He carried all of our sin, absorbed our hostility into Himself, even to the extent of death. In His very death He spoke back the word of love and acceptance. He carried His own indignation, His own wrath on our sin.

In his book, *The Meaning of the Cross,* H. E. W. Turner says, "While forgiveness was eternally implicit in the love of God, the cross became the fitting instrument through which that forgiveness was actualized to the sons of men."[1] Christ, in the middle of history, expressed the forgiveness that was in the heart of God from the dawn of creation. And now we can come to Him and be freed, freed from our estrangement and guilt because He forgives and accepts us.

Such forgiveness has a quality seldom expressed in our relations. Often in our humanness and pride, the best we can do is express tolerance. We don't really forgive and free the person— we only tolerate him. On our part this is the ultimate expression of pride, for the other this is the ultimate insult. Tolerance implies that a person should be satisfied when you permit him in your presence even though you keep him at your feet. Not only does this cause personal difficulties, but it also causes much of our class struggle, our racial difficulties, and our international resentments.

At the bottom of the conceited life is the quest for greatness. Jesus answered this among His disciples by asking for a conversion to the spirit of childlikeness. With such a spirit we are well aware of our dependence upon another. But we have failed, and until we deal honestly with our own sins, we will continue to be critical of others. Paul adds, "As God for Christ's sake forgave you, so also do ye." The honest admission of our own faults should lead us to forgive others who stumble. In this admission we can experience the forgiving of our inner self. To forgive one's self means accepting the humbling fact that we are less than our ideal, and calling the inner self to transformation.

[1]H. E. W. Turner, *The Meaning of The Cross* (London: A. R. Mowbray and Company; New York: Morehouse-Gorham Co., 1959).

To tolerate another as a substitute for forgiving is to continue the basic estrangement. Christian faith means a new quality of fellowship, a brotherhood of the forgiven. Here, we do not live with tolerance of one another, but in common acceptance that all are forgiven sinners. Tolerance can respect another's position and faith, but it doesn't achieve a covenant of common commitment. The covenant people are not a club of persons with naturally good dispositions but a company of the redeemed—the Church.

Forgiveness is always in relationship. It is not a commodity that one gets and runs away with. It is the acceptance of the guilty at a cost to the forgiving one. To quote H. E. W. Turner again, "Restoration of fellowship, whether with God or among men, can only be at a cost. Here no force is more creative or more potent in its effects than vicarious suffering. In human relationships no less than in God's dealing with men, to love is to suffer, and to suffer is to love."

To love is to accept another, open one's life to another. Love and forgiveness are inseparable aspects of interpersonal relationships. Interpersonal relations always involve the acceptance of persons who are imperfect. Love makes possible forgiving one who has done wrong, for love enables the forgiving one to carry his own wrath on the other's sin, freeing the guilty. One does not humiliate the other first and then accept him; this is not forgiveness, this is satisfying one's ego and then dismissing the case. Forgiveness is costly, it is resolving within one's self, by love, the indignation another's sin provokes and accepting the other in freedom. The forgiven one knows that he is accepted on the basis of another's grace. It is no wonder that the prophet said, "There is forgiveness with Thee that Thou mayest be feared." Knowing our own failings, we recognize that we can only enjoy relationship with Him if He forgives!

The full evidence that God has forgiven us is in the gift of the

Holy Spirit. God's acceptance is so complete that He dwells within us. Peter's sermon at Pentecost announced that by repenting and being baptized for remission of sins the believer would receive the Holy Spirit. Paul wrote to the Corinthians that being bought with the price of Christ's blood we are God's possession, and our very bodies become the temple of the Holy Spirit. Throughout the scope of Scripture the ultimate expression of salvation is God in the midst of His people. Reconciliation has an inner witness, the experience of the indwelling Holy Spirit now. He testifies that we have been adopted into God's family as sons.

~ 13 ~

What does it mean to say "yes," to affirm, to commit one's self? Is the day of the one hundred percenter past? Do men no longer want to commit themselves? Christ still asks for commitment, for one to take a stand for Him. And the New Testament places more emphasis on confessing Christ than it does on confessing sin! If one confesses Christ, that is, identifies with Him in life, he will confess or identify with God's rejection of sin. Confessing Christ as Lord comes first, not the negation of the mediocracies of life— that will follow.

Yes—As Big As Life

Much of modern life is empty boredom. John Steinbeck has said, "Having too much, we spend our time on psychiatrist's couches in search of a soul." We fail to find a sense of purpose and live in frustration and folly. The biography of many is, "Hurry, worry, bury!" Even in a good work our egos trick us by three temptations—"to shine, to recline, and then to whine." The horizons of our lives are too limited. Man is in search but seems never to find.

The Gospel has an answer, but it is costly. If Christ is Lord, we are to be His subject, living by His will. He calls us to take up our cross and follow Him, to step out of our meager existence into His fullness. This is a call for action, to live on the victory side of the cross, to be where the real action is. He asks for a "yes" as big as life.

Paul said his gospel was not "yes, yes, and no, no" (II Cor. 1:17); not a set of answers to multitudes of questions, but a great "yes" to God. In fact, if one's yes to God is big enough, it will cover the other questions in life. God in grace has said "yes" to man. He said it in the resurrection after man had said a deeply hostile "no" to Him. This is God's grace, accepting us that He might change us. Man's faith is a response to grace; it is man saying "yes" to God. Faith is a "yes" attitude which permits God to be Himself in one's life.

And this "yes" works in life. It is positive, decisive action. Neglect is enough to spoil human character. It doesn't take active wickedness to do so. The foolish virgins neglected their lamps. The travelers on the road to Jericho who passed by the wounded man did no more than pass by. The buried talent simply was not used. The old commandments, "Thou shalt not," have given way to the new commandments, "Thou shalt." Our greater sin is in having opportunity to do good and doing nothing.

Actually, it is expressing our "yes" to God before men which constitutes our witness. No one witnesses of Christ as Lord apart from exhibiting that he himself is saying, "Thy will be done on earth as it is done in heaven." The believer witnesses to being a member of the kingdom of heaven now. He is a "stranger and pilgrim" here influencing the world for God as he touches it. Jesus said in sending out His disciples, "Say unto them, the kingdom of God is come nigh unto you."

But this "yes" is not to a God far away, but to a God who is present in the person of the Holy Spirit. The God who confronts man in history, who came to man in Jesus Christ, has come to us in the Holy Spirit. The ultimate aspect of our salvation experience is not in being forgiven but is in being given the Holy Spirit. The Holy Spirit is God present with us! The promise of the Father and the promise of Christ is one—the gift of the Spirit to indwell the life of the believer and by Him to be made a member of the "body of Christ." Paul writes, "By one Spirit are we all baptized into one body" (1 Cor. 12:13).

A person does not say "yes" simply in the primary experience of conversion. It is an attitude of life. A disciple is one who continues to say "yes" to his Lord. One of the problems of Protestantism is a fear of obedience lest it be "works righteousness." We need to recognize the difference between works of merit and works of faith. Works of merit are attempts to win or earn God's approval, while works of faith are expressions of identification with the Christ. Legalism works toward the cross, but discipleship works from the cross. When we have said "yes" to God's call of grace, have identified with Him, our discipleship is the expression in life of the difference He makes.

∾ 14 ∾

"The fruit of the Spirit is . . . JOY."
(Gal. 5:22)
"The JOY of the Lord shall be your
strength." (Neh. 8:10)
"The kingdom of heaven is . . . JOY in
the Holy Spirit." (Rom. 14:17)
"I will JOY in the God of my salva-
tion." (Hab. 3:18)
"Your JOY no man taketh from you."
(Jo. 16:22)
". . . Jesus Christ, whom having not
seen ye love; in whom, though now ye
see Him not, yet believing, ye rejoice
with JOY unspeakable and full of
glory." (1 Pet. 1:8)

Joy in the Spirit

Joy is a quality of life which transcends pleasure. While you may derive pleasure from things, you get joy from wholesome relationships. Joy has to do with one's spirit, one's inner man, one's mood. It makes one radiant and companionable. It enriches lives by the delight of a healthy spirit. It is the reward that comes when life is in harmony with divine purpose.

Joy is a fruit of the Spirit, shared when one's spirit is affected by His presence. Such is Paul's definition of the kingdom of heaven . . . "Righteousness, peace, and joy in the Holy Spirit." There is significance to the order here; righteous, meaning right relation, peace, the absence of a disturbing factor, and joy, the delight of true fulfillment. There is no joy for the meager soul lacking the fulfillment of its highest capacities. With potential to think God's thoughts, to share God's work, man cannot know joy at lesser levels of life. He only shares a shriveled, ego-enslaved soul.

Joy is therapy of soul, for when it is known, the soul experiences refinement.

Joy is the strength of life, for a man at peace in himself shares the greater power of life.

Joy is the cadence which brings the music of harmony to the fore in the experiences of life.

The wise man said, "Cast sadness far from thee, because it has killed many and is good for nothing." Usually, the unhappy man tries to escape from himself in excitement, stimulants, and erotic experiences. But overcoming sadness begins with understanding it. Sad people are saying, "I do not respect myself." We must remove the battleground between our higher self and our lower self. Does your higher self looks down on your lower self with disgust. Only when you put God between you and your sinful life can you enjoy yourself. By faith we can refuse to assent to the poverty of our own personality.

To pass from sadness to joy takes a work of God, it takes a birth of love, an experience of forgiveness and inner healing. Joy is the delight of love, it comes from within while pleasure comes from without. In the joy of the Spirit our own spirit is lifted, our disposition is enriched.

When we are sad, we are guilty of unbelief, of failing to recognize God. We can do something about sadness—what is outside us may be beyond our control, but what is inside can be

brought under His control. Our lives are transformed in humble
recognition of God's presence. Humility is not to look down on
ourselves, but to look away from ourselves to the Greater. Here
is the source of joy—to be caught up in a purpose so much greater
than our's that we are free from selfishness. Luke describes Jesus
as rejoicing in spirit that the knowledge of God was revealed to
common men.

Only when we have a happy conscience can we have a happy
outlook. Good humor is the spirit of joy. As Christians, we need
a sense of humor, not taking ourselves too seriously, and having a
joyous delight in God's purpose. The disciplined life has dis-
covered that happiness is not found in indulgence but in total
satisfaction—"In Thy presence is fulness of joy." In surrender to
the will of God, we have the inner satisfaction of belonging, of
being at rest. Accepting His grace of reconciliation, there is the
joyous assurance of being participants in eternal life. The writer
of Hebrews says, "There remaineth therefore a rest to the people
of God, for he that is entered into rest, he also hath ceased from
his own works, as God did from his." We who believe have found
that there is "joy and peace in believing."

❦ 15 ❦

Love means that one's life is
intimately open to another.
In loving God with our whole person
we open our total life to Him:
Our hearts—affections,
Our minds—attitudes,
Our souls—ambition,
Our strength—activity.
To love is costly, for it means
our complete participation in life.

The Difficulties of Love

Many young people today are cynical before they reach their teens. They know all the questions by the age of five and all the answers by the age of fifteen. What is left? And the common answer is, the search for love. But of what quality? A mere ego-satisfying endorsement in relation with another? Or a shallow, sentimental type, a surface affection. An attempt to satisfy the desires of the moment? We need an education of the spirit today as much as of the mind.

Genuine love would be an answer to much of our world's ills. True love is infused with the qualities of integrity, of wholeness, of giving, which enrich life. Most of what moderns call love is only "eros," a completely human quality which tends to use affection to cover up the selfish manipulation of another. Erotic love is the plucking of one string to the exclusion of all others. But there is a higher quality of love, a love that truly cares, that involves one's self for the benefit of another at cost to one's self. This is *agape* love, known only in grace. Such love touches the whole person. This is the love which "suffereth long and is kind, envieth not, does not behave itself unseemly."

One of the great values of love is its ability to endure; it lasts. Love survives where all else in human dignity would die. But, such love is difficult for a number of reasons. It is not easy to live in love, for love must grow. Love is not static; it cannot remain where it is. Beware of thinking you have arrived, for such is selfish and love will dissipate in your very hands. It is not easy to live in love because it must be constant. True love is always giving itself—it cares; it is involved; it shares—and this is one of the most costly aspects of life. It is not easy to live in love because it must be inclusive. The character of love calls us to serve, and service is not dependent upon the object itself. Moreover, it cannot and will not be partial. It is not easy to live in love because it must be creative. Love makes something of us; it changes us. In sharing love, we pay the price of change. Finally, it is not easy to live in love because it must move beyond the issue to the person. So often we hang up on the issue, we quarrel and experience estrangement from persons with whom we should share understanding and love. Love may be harsh for a moment, "Faithful are the wounds of a friend," but it is visible beyond the wound.

Love is not easy; it is difficult. But life does not come to any of us ready-made. Love is for the daring and the brave. It's demands are exciting, but they lie beyond the reach of the weakling or the coward. Love is strong, for it is an energy source; it is capable of propelling persons toward people or things. It is capable of making others love back; thus, it is a compliment to others; in turn, it makes us lovable.

What is the course of love when you are helping persons whose difficulties are character rather than circumstances? This is more difficult than when the need is material. Jesus would have us recognize that loving our neighbor as our self is to bring him to the most important dimension of life—character-changing faith. To love is to be an agent of reconciliation, to be the "priest at your brother's elbow," the one through whom God calls another to Himself. This is the deeper meaning of evangelism—not a sales-pitch, not dogmatic intolerance of another's position, not proselytization! Evangelism is witness of the transforming grace of Christ so that one may discover the better life in Him. "We preach not ourselves but Christ Jesus the Lord." Christian love seeks to introduce others to the Lord of the universe.

Love identifies; it does not condescend. Love stands alongside; it isn't an approach that stoops to others. In love, God came and stood with us, "bearing our sins in His own body on the tree," accepting our problems as His own. If we would help another, we must become involved with him, sharing first in understanding, in moral and spiritual support. The way of love is not to cover another person's needs for him, it is rather sharing with him. The impersonal nature of much of our charities and missions is an example of the difficulty of sharing in love. But we can begin where we are, believing in the power of love to influence others to live by love. One doesn't think of doing more himself than he can do well. One who lives by love believes in its power and seeks to stimulate others to live by this spirit. It will spread.

~ 16 ~

Is justice met when men strike back,
To balance one more score,
To repay the damage "tit for tat."
And promote revenge the more?

Does not justice cover more than acts,
Its scope all human kind,
Its aim correction of all ills,
The whole of human stride?

For mercy works in justice,
To correct that it may save
To turn a man himself from wrong
That he may yet behave.

Justice, the Virtue of Wrath

As Christians we are called to evangelism, but this is not the total of our mission to the world. We are also called to serve our fellows in binding up the wounded, building bridges between the estranged, creating a sense of brotherhood among peoples. Here we bring together evangelism and social action, defying the divorce created by church groups on either side. Is it not right for Christians to feel outraged over evil? Amos has been called "God's angry prophet." The church could profit from a few of his type.

To love is to care deeply, and in doing so we accept the cost of love. This cost may mean carrying our wrath on injustice into involvement! God didn't simply call down a word of concern from above, He involved Himself in our problem. He did this in a manner which exposed our sin and perversion rather than condoned it. At the same time, He worked to correct the perversion. It is the holy character of God's justice which makes justice the mediator between His wrath and His love.

God's wrath is actually His respect for our freedom to say "no" to Him. He made man in His image—free, but man enthroned himself and became enslaved by his sin. God now comes to man in sin with the freedom of grace. He offers forgiveness, life, and acceptance. But the freedom of grace has in it respect for man's freedom to keep saying "no" to God. Hell is God's irrevocable refusal to coerce a man to change his "no" even though it means He cannot accept the man who refuses to accept Him. God's wrath is His complement to man's freedom. The value of wrath is its refusal to ignore the seriousness of perversion and disharmony. Wrath can be a valid reaction against wrong. Christ got angry—but take note, His anger was focused primarily on issues, only by implication involving persons. If the issue can be exposed, we can often save the person.

Justice is the virtue of wrath for it is God's discretion in coping with perversion. Justice deals in relation to principles and is no respector of persons. True justice seeks to correct injustice; it isn't fulfilled by seeking to punish or by taking revenge. God in justice will take vengeance on the unbeliever; that is, He will apply the meaning of justice to the man's decision. But this is not revenge; this is not satisfying a wounded ego by striking back. God's justice works to achieve the larger good for a person. But in man's decision to say "no" to God, Divine justice respects man's freedom to say "no."

Virtue in wrath is the larger justice which cares deeply enough to give one's self in correcting the problem. God in Christ gave Himself. The universe will witness to the justice of how He has worked to cope with man's sin. Just so, we who believe are called to share His mission. It is right to be indignant about social evil. It is just to expose institutional structures which stifle real personhood. It is Christian to reject war and violence which supports the idolatry of nationalism at the expense of the Kingdom of Christ.

But beware, lest in seeing virtue in wrath you develop a climate of self-defense, and a spirit of negativism. Justice seeks the larger good. When true to its deepest character, it is constructive, not negative. It is easy to picket, to demonstrate, but it is more difficult to be creative and constructive. How does one correct the inequities between peoples where the rich become richer and the poor become poorer? How can we repay privileges lost to people by the tyranny of slavery or the ravages of war? Is it not our Christian responsibility to work for better education, better health facilities, better housing, and a better understanding of social and personal ethics? And yet, while working at all of these, we must recognize the deeper cause of man's perversion. Justice works to correct injustice toward God and man. If we would counteract the problems of sin, we must seek to correct the sinner.

❧ 17 ❧

Each person carries some type of moral atmosphere,

> *Exerts some influence upon others.*
What kind of people are attracted to you?

> *Are people comfortable in your presence?*
Are you fun to live with?

> *Are you an enjoyable friend?*
Do you influence others for God and good?

> *Can you help one find His peace?*
Isaiah says: "They helped everyone his neighbor,

> *And everyone said to his brother,*
> *Be of good courage." (Isa. 41:6)*

Influence for Good

Many persons tend to live in the abstract to avoid concrete responsibility. We forget that "none of us liveth to himself and no man dieth to himself." Each of us carries a "moral atmosphere" which enriches or degrades the lives of those we touch. Let each of us ask, "What kind of persons are attracted to me or enjoy being in my presence?" Or again, "What effect have I had in the past year upon those closest to me?" Or simply, "Am I pleasant to live with?"

Some seek to avoid their responsibility for positive action, being satisfied with a boast of being honest. In fact, honesty has become a "shibboleth," a password, often used as an excuse for mediocrity. But honesty is not enough! Some say, "Don't be a hypocrite, if you have wrong thoughts or desires express them. Not only is this a sell-out—a denial of the value of inner personal discipline—the answer is too easy. Does this mean that if one feels lust he should commit adultry, or if one feels indignation he should commit murder, or if one feels like swearing he should poison the mood and minds of others?

Honesty without a commitment of faith has no saving power. It may be a cover-up for pride, for one's God-almightiness, a twisted phoniness! Being honest may mean you are a "self," but it doesn't say what kind of self. It takes more than honesty to be noble, upright, and saintly. Honesty must witness to something beyond one's self, an enriching fellowship with Christ.

Our influence for good in the world is our witness of what Christ is doing in our own lives. Should someone question the importance of conversion, let us witness to what it means in our experience. Should someone doubt the reality of the Spirit-filled life, let us witness to what He means within us. If there is a question on the validity of faith, let us demonstrate it in the values of prayer.

The only meaningful way of promoting morality is by example. To live a life of moral integrity outweighs all the words which might be spoken. Our lives must give evidence that we use the product which we are trying to sell. The generation has given rise to multiple groups who explain their own perversions by telling us they didn't find love and integrity at home. Faith must be lived if it is to be recognized as relevant. In Christ, a person is a new creature—it is of primary importance that we discover how the new creature is to conduct himself.

True religion is not expressed fully inside the four walls of a church building. We must take our faith home from church. The greater expression of worship is in the daily praise of the committed life. Salvation is not something we possess, as an insurance policy; it is participation with Christ in a life of discipleship. Each day provides us with opportunities to express the meaning of Christ's Lordship. The social expressions of the Gospel are the application of evangelical faith to the whole of life. The whole person is being brought to Christ. We are not saving "souls" as mystical entities, but persons who are "living souls." All of life is important with God, for life is the arena in which we evidence our faith.

Man has tied to him the price tag of Calvary. According to the Bible, God counts every man worth the death of Deity. The Scripture stresses the ultimate importance of man. It provides us with the highest view of human nature. As believers, we know each other in grace, recognizing the spiritual potential of the other. We share with God in bringing a redemptive influence upon each individual with whom we associate. Recognizing that the Holy Spirit doesn't work in a vacuum, we yield ourselves to His Mastery so He can touch others through us. Beyond the church, this means witness and service in the name of Christ. Within the church, this means involvement and constructive support. At levels where the church needs correction, we are like Kierkegaard, "Carrying on an unhappy love-affair with the Church." We find our first responsibility in the Kingdom to be in the local church fellowship.

Today, many are down-grading the church and failing to see its influence for good in society. Of course, the church is imperfect; it is made up of imperfect people. Even the early church had an Annanias and Sapphira who sought credit for a dedication they weren't living up to; a Diotrophese who loved to have the preeminence; and a Demas who went back to the world. However, the failures are far more than matched by successes in grace. We need to assume more responsibility for the Church, to overcome the cultural lag, and to become a transforming influence in culture. We need to have a firm grasp on a sound philosophy of life, a close relationship with common people, and a criticism which is hard on ourselves and easy on others. As we share, we can help our local congregation to become a vital, active force for good in our community.

∽ 18 ∽

In Reformation faith there are four major principles:
—The sole authority of Scripture, "sola scriptura."
—Justification by faith, "sola fide."
—The Priesthood of all believers,
—The sanctity of all of life!

The latter has been minimized in the life of the church. We have yet to discover the full meaning of "Christian vocation," of bringing the common life under the sovereign will of the Spirit of Christ.

The Impact of Sanctity

Secularization has initiated some of the greatest opportunities and some of the greatest problems in the history of man. While it accounts for our technological advance, it easily turns us to the idolatory of secularism. In the latter, man is placed at the center of life instead of God, anthropology is made the queen of the sciences instead of theology. Our technology is becoming our master. The story is told of the development of a most intricate computer, which, when fed the question, "Is there a

God?" came out with the answer, "If there wasn't before, there is now."

In a technological society there is a resultant depersonalization. Consequently, there is no vital acting community. There is the difficult problem of getting next to people. In this society the church becomes a copy rather than a conscience. We are more diplomatic than disciplined. We are parasites instead of prophets, for many people have no internal signals. Many persons succumb to the status quo and become hollow individuals. With sub-Christian levels of behavior we tend to pervert the expression of the Gospel and fail to enrich our society. How will men come to believe? If Christ can't call the best out of persons, He doesn't merit their worship! But He can. There isn't an area of life that isn't enriched when brought under the Lordship of Christ.

It is a part of our Christian mission to bring the secular into focus with the sacred. The sacred is not a retreat from the secular. God created a good world. The Bible says, "The Word was made flesh and dwelt among us;" the Incarnation thereby demonstrating that matter is not evil in itself. Are we not called to discipleship? to responsible and holy behavior in life? Do we not affirm our faith in the resurrection, meaning that God is not through with this creation? As Christians we are to bring the influence of the sacred to bear upon the secular now. In so doing we can keep the secular from claiming wholeness for itself. Life is not whole apart from God. We can expose the tendency of the secular to idolatry, of being an end in itself. But in doing this we must avoid a monasticism which renounces the secular. Our use of the secular is conditioned by our participation in grace, for "to the pure all things are pure."

A further aspect of our mission is for the sacred to prevent the perversions of the secular. In his book, *Honest Religion For*

Secular Man, Lesslie Newbigin says, "If the mastery which is given to man through the process of secularization is not held within the context of man's responsibility to God, the result will be a new slavery."[1] Moving in the secular, it is easy to permit the fully secular to provide the framework for life. This is all right for the state, for a good government is secular, not trying to speak for God, protecting the church to do that. But a secular church is a fallen church. Anything that has only itself as a frame of reference will disintegrate. The Church lives by the directive of its Lord and challenges the state not to disregard the highest authority. Christianity has improved the world by providing it something of superior quality to relate to. This improvement often happens even when a society rejects faith, for it is still influenced by the better which it will not fully accept.

Finally, we must regard the secular as the realm in which we evidence the sacred. In "the Word became flesh," we are provided exhibit number one for this thesis. We are responsible to make our faith visible to others. Jesus said, "Inasmuch as ye have done it unto one of the least of these, my brethren, ye have done it unto me." We must remind ourselves that relevance is not determined by what *is* but by what *ought to be*. We are to be the "salt of the earth," "the light of the world." As has been said, "You don't use salt to salt salt!" The church is to be in the world as Jesus was in the world, yet not of the world. The way to achieve this type of relationship is to live in the world with a mission which comes from beyond the world. Our mission in the secular age is to point secular man beyond himself to a meaningful relation with One who is wholly Other. As we live now under the Lordship of Christ, we show to our society the reality of the spiritual Kingdom.

---

[1] Lesslie Newbigin, *Honest Religion for Secular Man* (London: SCM Press, Ltd., 1966).

The nature of faith is to stimulate faith. In a secular age the Church is facing the greatest test of her faith. Can we so live by faith that others will discover faith in Christ? This is our ultimate mission. Put this first, and other areas of Christianized service will follow; put humanitarian concerns first and faith in Christ will be eclipsed by faith in man. Brunner has said, "The church exists by mission as fire exists by burning." Let us witness to a faith that is in contact with God. Secular man will respect the sacred when we show him the Christ who is available for encounter in his moment of faith.

*Jesus said, "My kingdom is not of this
world, for if my kingdom were of this
world then would my servants fight
that I should not be delivered unto the
Jews, but now is my kingdom not from
hence."*

*To share a kingdom of spirit, a com-
munity of spirit, and a style of life that
is spiritual is to recognize the "spirit
nature of man" and see the correction
of his problems in a transformation
which begins with man's inner being,
with his "core-worth."*

Members of His Kingdom

Man was made not for one world but for two. The kingdom
of heaven is a present spiritual reality in which Christ as Lord
gathers His members. This is an eschatological reality, but as
such, it is not solely future. We live now in relation to that which
we know will ultimately come. Jesus said, "The kingdom cometh
not with observation," and again "the kingdom is within you."
But He also speaks of His kingdom coming, and of delivering
His completed kingdom over to the Father for all eternity. He

came to introduce this kingdom in the world and call us to kingdom membership.

To belong truly to Christ is to be a member of His kingdom now. We are to be citizens of heaven while here in this world. Actually, we are strangers and pilgrims looking for an eternal city. As such we do not seek our security in this life. We give ourselves in service to our fellows so that they may sense the call to kingdom membership. We face a modern man, less and less bound by history. For him change is more real than continuity. He needs a new sense of piety in relation to the higher will of Christ, a sense of being other-world oriented. With such a perspective, we can keep our heads when others are obsessed by fear. A man once ran up to Edison crying, "What will we do, the world is coming to an end!" Edison's calm reply was, "We can get along all right without it!"

Kingdom membership transcends earthly nationalism and makes possible the universal nature of the Church. Powers of state, according to Paul's letter to the Romans, stand under God, and as servants in His order they are to protect the innocent and punish the evil. But take note, the powers are *under* God; He is the one Highest Power. There are many times that the Christian will need to say, "We ought to obey God rather than men." No member of the kingdom of heaven can obey the state in levels of sub-Christian action and expect his disloyalty to the lordship of Christ to be overlooked. For example, the fact that the state asks participation does not free the Christian's conscience from the guilts of war. We who know Christ cannot let a secondary authority annul His authority for our lives. Our mission is not fulfilled at the level of earthly structures; it is a mandate to "make disciples of all men." Paul says that our Lord stands above "all principalities, and powers, and might, and dominion," that the world may know through the Church the nature of His eternal purpose. Society, national strength, is but the scaffolding for the Church which works redemptively within society. Things have come to a spiritual impasse when the Church operates under the mandate of society. Where is our freedom, our boldness to operate under the authority of our Lord, His Word, and His Spirit?

In freedom from the idolatry of secularism, the kingdom member will live under the direction of the Holy Spirit. The Christ, who baptizes with the Spirit, gives the Spirit to those who take Him as Lord. It is the intent of the Spirit to fill us with His influence and power. By His power He carries us beyond the limitations of ourselves. Each day we will seek to discover what the Spirit would teach us, both through the brotherhood and through crises experiences in the world. Standing in "Christ," we interpret life in this world by the principles from the other.

Each of us is called to declare his loyalty in life. When we have been translated "from the kingdom of darkness into the kingdom of His Son," it is reflected in our total life. The believer's role is service to the One he confesses as Lord. In this service we are "predestined to be conformd to the image of His Son." Under the sovereign will of the Spirit, we are called to live, by the norm of Christ, a life sensitive to His direction.

Our mission is now to extend the arms of the Church around the world, to be universal Christians. Faith in Christ will lead to greater international involvement in faith, to our being "a people for His name." His kingdom is to be a universal expression of the fellowship of the Spirit, transcending earthly national and racial boundaries. With Christ every individual is of equal value, all men equally count with God, and there is no Christian nation as such. Let us beware of placing institutions above persons. We must remember that the person transcends every community. When the Church lives with the cross at its heart, it will not hold itself above the individual. As members of His kingdom, we are each "members one of another," (Eph. 4:25b).

~ 20 ~

The path of life has many branches:
  One can turn to left or right,
Decisions face one ever and again;
  But these decisions become simpli-
  fied,
  If one has made the basic decision—
  direction!

Jesus said: "Enter ye in at the strait
gate: for wide is the gate and broad
is the way, that leadeth to destruc-
tion, and many there be which go in
thereat: Because strait is the gate,
and narrow is the way, which
leadeth unto life, and few there be
that find it."

Where is the "narrow way"? where
does one find it? The broad way is
the stream of humanity with its back
turned on God—the narrow way is
right in the middle of the broad
way, only it is heading in the other
direction!

Decision

One of the greatest gifts in life is the freedom to make decisions. This is a gift God has given us in grace. Recognizing the
conditioning aspects of heredity and environment, or the psychological and sociological factors of decision making, it appears

that humanly speaking most of life is determined for us. This would be so except for Christ. His coming to us makes possible a decision for God. This third dimension makes decision possible. Hopeless man is introduced to a relationship with Christ, to a new birth—the beginning of a new life.

In the understanding of human personality it becomes evident that man needs to be converted. One psychologist has said, "We are so psychologically constituted as to need converting, and if the church fails to convert people, we psychologists are going to have to do it." Fulton Sheen quips, "A flat tire cannot fix itself!" Only Christ can change human nature. The confrontation brought about by His Spirit makes this decision of faith possible.

Decision making does involve more than an original choice to follow Christ. In one sense, as the Reformers said, all of life is a repentance. This means that the evidence of Christ's Lordship in one's life is the recognition of His will in daily decisions. All of life involves selectivity. We cannot avoid this, for we can't do everything that is possible in the field of choice. In our choices we express our true character and the principles by which we live. One mark of maturity is when we move beyond deciding simply on the basis of good and bad to decide between the good, better, or best!

Our decisions carry the weight of our future. And they must be made before we know the full results. How important to deliberate, to decide by principles proven in life. And yet, so much is decided in faith. As one decision leads on to another, we continue to change. We are never the same. By the very nature of life we are in the process of becoming. Each of us will be what he is becoming—but each one is becoming what he will be? This is the seriousness of decision. The paths which call for our choice now may be close together, but as they lead on they become far apart. Like the entrance to a throughway, the driver chooses and his destination follows, but at the point of choice it would have been easy to have gone either way. So in life, Christ confronts us: "Yoke yourself with Me," he cries, and makes choice both possible and necessary.

It is psychologically true that when a person confronts you decision is inescapable. One either chooses to give acceptance or rejection. God confronts us in His written Word, in propositions with which we may debate; but He confronts us in Christ, the living Word as Person, and here debate is only a facade over the real decision to accept or reject Him. In our decision we either come to know Him or we turn from Him. In the decision to know Him we discover that He comes to us in the Person of the Holy Spirit, and our decision is a response. But not once only, for response is an attitude. To know a person well, there must be association, expression and response. By constant interaction, by communion with the Holy Spirit, by conversing with Him, we discover more about Him and more about ourselves. Each discovery enables a further decision and enhances our achievements. Step by step one yields as much of himself as he understands to as much of God as he understands.

Too frequently we are caught in the ambiguities of life and· fail to act decisively. When one finds himself both loving God for meeting religious needs and hating God for religious demands, he is spiritually neurotic. The result is, to say the least, spiritual atrophy. Such indecision is seen in the plight of the woman who was asked by her psychiatrist, "Do you have trouble making decisions?" to which she responded, "Well . . . yes, and no . . ."

The person who has made the inner choice of integrity will find it easy to be completely honest in difficult experiences. Having made the decision to walk with God, all lesser decisions are easier and clearer. One who has an inner appreciation for freedom will be concerned about tyranny and slavery. Knowing inner discipline and victory, we can share helpfully with the defeated. The decision for Christ frees the ego from seeking satisfaction by satiating itself. It has been said, "A hungry ego is a mean ego." When one is on good terms with God, he can be on good terms with himself and with others. A person has to lower himself if he is to be petty in relation to others.

Man is made for eternity, to share the ages with God in ongoing fulfillment. Life for the Christian takes on this quality of eternity now. We live as belonging already to the eternal spheres. Anticipating the return of our Lord, we know that history will not end with a "whimper" or "a bang," but history is a part of God's program, the triumph of which is ultimately beyond time. Decisions for Christ, to identify with Him in discipleship, is to make decisions today in relation to their ultimate meaning.

Christian decision should, above all else, mean Christian vocation. We fulfill our calling best when we influence others to open their lives to God and become participants in His work. This is living "after the power of an endless life." In our decision of faith we are saying "yes" to God and "yes" to His kind of life. We have decided to be God's kind of man. In decision we affirm our participation in His program, our membership on His team. This means that we live now in the light of Christ's return and the ultimate glory. With this long-range goal in view our short-range involvements are in better perspective.

To find our way out of the wood's when we're lost, we do not simply sight one tree and move toward it, but we should align it with another farther on. To aim a gun, we need not only a near sight beyond the stock but a farther one on the end of the barrel. To succeed in life, we need more than the immediate goal; we should align the present with our ultimate goal beyond.